PODCAST MASTERY: SPECIAL REPORT

Contents

Introduction

In case you haven't heard much about podcasting, let me tell you a little bit about it, and how it's commonly used by business professionals.

Think of podcasting as somewhat like a radio talk show, only podcasts aren't typically broadcast live. They are usually pre-recorded, edited, and then uploaded. Sometimes they CAN be live shows that are recorded and uploaded later, but that's far less common.

Podcasts can be set to download automatically by fans of that podcast, and can be listened to anytime, from any location, as long as internet is available to download the podcast at some point before listening.

Podcasts are a great way to stay in touch with your audience, while also expanding it quickly. Millions of users listen to podcasts every day, and you can reach a large number of those users quickly and easily.

In fact, Pat Flynn of the Smart Passive Income blog, says that his podcast has become his top method for reaching new customers and generating fresh traffic to his website, ranking podcasting's global outreach above Google, social media, and inbound links!

As a result of his podcasts, Pat has received lots of media coverage and opportunities that probably would not have been open to him if he hadn't started his podcast.

Wouldn't you like to have that kind of exposure?

Then let's get started!

Podcasting 101

Podcasts are an incredible way to reach both current and new prospects, no matter what type of business you're running, or what niche market you are positioned in.

Podcasting is also a great way to stand out, and set yourself apart from the competition. Lots of people have blogs and YouTube channels and social media profiles, but not nearly as many people have a podcast!

There are around 100 million people who listen to podcasts every single day, but only about 200,000 active podcasts. Compare that to the millions of active blogs out there!

Podcast readership is also still growing. Between 2015 and 2016 alone, listeners grew by a whopping **23%**!

Podcasting is a fantastic way to gain exposure for your blog, YouTube channel, social media profiles, books, courses, brand, app, software, video game, or anything else you're working on!

Plus, it's a great way to gain exposure for people who aren't as comfortable in front of a camera. People never have to know what you look like. And even if you hate your voice, you could use a voice changer to modify it!

But don't think you have to have a fantastic voice to do well with a podcast. As long as you have something interesting to say, listeners will keep tuning in.

Whatever you're trying to accomplish with your business—whether it's selling products, getting readers for your blog or books, getting views to your YouTube videos, or building your brand—you can achieve it with podcasting!

Types of Podcasts

There are many different types of podcasts you can create for your audience, and nothing says you need to stay with a single format. In fact, **lots** of people use multiple formats for their podcast based on whatever they are trying to accomplish at a given time.

Let's take a look at some of those different formats, and how they can best be used.

Solo

Most podcasts are solo, simply because it's usually individuals who start them. Solo podcasts generally consist of one individual talking about a particular subject during each "episode".

Duos

Duos are also popular, with two people talking together about the topic. Duos are often spouses or friends, but may be business partners, or other close acquaintances.

The reason most duos are close is that their personalities need to mesh well for the podcast to be interesting.

Duos need to feed off each other, joke around with each other, and be able to read each other to understand where the other one is going with the conversation and respond thoughtfully.

Interviews

Interview based podcasts typically involve two people. One, the host asks questions, and the other party provides information and shares their strategies, and experiences within the podcast.

The interview format is a simple one: The host provides a set list of questions ahead of time, giving their guest a chance to review the material and prepare for the episode. Just like in any other podcast scenario, it's always best to have a pre-written outline of what you plan to cover within the podcast, as well as opening and closing remarks.

Interview based podcasts can work especially well if you manage to get well-known people in your industry to participate, because those established names can draw in additional listeners, and they may even promote your podcast to their own fans or followers.

Groups

The group format can be tricky, because powerful personalities often have difficulty taking a backstage to each other and tend to talk over one another and interrupt. But they can be very successful if they are properly moderated.

If you've ever watched a show like *Real Time with Bill Maher* or *The View*, you've pretty much seen how interesting, and dynamic this type of format can be.

The group format isn't as common in podcasting because of the need to moderate so many personalities and because of potential scheduling conflicts, but they can be quite successful if executed correctly.

As I mentioned before, you don't have to stick to a single format. You might run your podcast as a single format most of the time, and switch to other formats here and there, or you might switch it up all the time. It's totally up to you, and what you hope to accomplish.

If you are just getting started with podcasts, you'll likely want to start with just a solo podcast format. That way, you can cut your teeth on the process involved in creating great podcast content, gain experience and become more comfortable speaking to your audience.

Then, as you become more familiar with the process and feel prepared to try a new format, consider the interview-style format where you can welcome a guest from within your niche market to appear on your podcast. It's a great way to network with others in your industry while giving your listeners helpful information that will motivate them to continue tuning in each week, or month.

Plus, with interviews, you aren't required to come up with as much content as you would in a solo-format. You simply create a list of questions and let your guest provide the answers. In exchange for them appearing on your podcast, you could promote one of their products or website. It's a win-win!

Getting Started With Your First Podcast

A lot of people mistakenly believe that they need special equipment in order to create a podcast, but the truth is, you probably already have most of what you need on your computer.

Here's what you need:

- A computer
- A microphone
- Some sort of recording software
- Audio editing software (optional)

- Domain
- Hosting

Let's take a closer look at each piece of equipment you need, so you can get started quickly and easily.

Computer

You don't need the world's most powerful computer to create a podcast. Working with audio isn't nearly as intensive as working with graphics or video, so a basic computer is fine.

Technically, you can even create a podcast on your phone or tablet using software such as *BossJock Studio*. It's one of the only apps on the market that will allow you to record two mics at the same time, and if you plan to do any interviews, you'll need this feature. It's a very affordable app, and you can upload and publish your content as an MP3 file directly from the app.

Microphone

Many people just use the built-in microphone that comes with their computer or mobile device, and that's fine when you're just getting started. But the sound quality will probably not be what you want it to be.

Built-in microphones are generally low quality and will pick up too much ambient noise, and may include annoying artifacts such as static, hissing, wind, etc. This will hurt the overall quality of your podcast considerably, especially for people wearing earbuds or headphones.

Instead, it's recommended that you pick up an external microphone--ideally one that has a stand, noise reduction, and a windscreen or pop filter.

A pop filter is a shield that attaches to the microphone and blocks any air from your mouth and nose from reaching the mic, which will help reduce wind noise when you're speaking. Since it sits between you and the microphone, it won't block ambient airflow from other directions.

A windscreen is usually made of foam and fits over the mic itself to help reduce wind from all directions. This is useful for blocking wind when you're recording outdoors, but will also reduce noise from fans, air conditioning, etc.

You can buy pop filters and windscreens separately if your device doesn't come with them. If you aren't ready to invest in these accessories, you can also cover it loosely with a tissue or thin cloth to help reduce wind. It won't be as effective as a paid product, but it will help some.

There are many different types of microphones on the market. The least expensive models are generally not very good, but you don't have to spend hundreds of dollars to get a quality mic.

Let's take a look at a few models you might want to consider.

NEAT Widget

The NEAT Widget line of microphones runs in the $100 range and currently comes in three different models. They are all basically the same. The only real differences are cosmetic, so it just depends on which model you like.

At this price range, there isn't much that can beat it, and you'll see that the reviews on websites like Amazon prove it. These mics record very high-quality audio, do a great job of blocking ambient noise, and pick up voices like a champ.

Blue Yeti

The Blue Yeti microphone is pretty much the standard in podcasting. It's about 50% pricier than the NEAT Widget line if you purchase one of the models that comes with a pop filter and headphones, but a lot of people say it's worth the extra cost.

Blue Snowball iCE

The Blue Snowball iCE is another quality microphone that comes it at only about $50. This is a good option if you're looking to start podcasting on a budget, because of its affordable price, but be aware that it does tend to pick up more background noise than the NEAT Widget and Blue Yeti models.

You might think this won't matter much, because you'll be recording in a private space, however it can pick up noises such as air conditioners, squeaky chairs, rustling papers, etc. If this isn't a big deal for you, this model might be a good option.

iRig Mic Lav

If you want to record on the go, or if you think you might move around while you record your podcast, you might want to consider the iRig Mic Lav.

This device records quality sound with a mobile device, and you can even chain them so you can record with two mics at once for interviews. These even come in a convenient two-pack on some sites like Amazon, so you can purchase two at once and get a discount off the single unit price.

Since a lot of podcasters also record videos or do live video broadcasts, this particular model can be especially useful.

Recording & Editing Software

For editing, you can use something like TwistedWave.
(https://twistedwave.com/)

TwistedWave is available for Mac, iPhone and iPad, or it can even be used online if you don't have any Apple devices with any major web browser such as Safari, Firefox, Chrome, and IE.

If you already have a subscription to Adobe Creative Cloud, you can use Adobe Audition to edit your audio files. Audition is one of the best audio editing software packages around, you can record directly into the software, even if you're using something like Skype to conduct interviews via the internet.

Of course, Adobe CC can be a pricey option at about fifty bucks a month, or twenty just for Audition, so you might want something a little cheaper.

If you have a Mac or iOS device, you can use GarageBand. You won't have the range of options available to you that you would with Audition, but it will work for beginners.

Another great option is Audacity. (http://audacity.sourceforge.net/) Audacity is free, and you can both record and edit inside it. It's not as powerful as Audition, but it's free, and it is available for Windows, Mac and Linux operating systems.

Domain & Hosting

Yes, you will need to have your own hosting to run your podcast. You might be thinking that it would be hosted on iTunes or other podcast systems, but your podcasts are actually hosted elsewhere. Think of those services more as search engines or content aggregators than hosts.

It's highly recommended that you do NOT host your podcast directly on your own web hosting, because if it becomes slow, you could lose listeners. It can also be expensive to host those files on your own server.

Instead, you can use a service like Libsyn (http://libsyn.com) or Buzzsprout (http://buzzsprout.com) to host your podcasts. You upload your podcasts to your chosen podcast host, NOT directly to iTunes and other services.

Instead, you upload your podcast FEED to those directories. We'll talk more about distributing your podcast feed in the next section.

It's also a very good idea to have a website to host your podcast, because you will want to have a place to send your podcast traffic to convert them into email subscribers, leads, or sales.

Most people choose to have a blog, which is perfect for podcasting because you can have an opt-in form to generate leads, you can post on your blog whenever you release a new podcast, and you can post articles there as well.

Distributing
Your Podcast

As I mentioned earlier, you don't upload your podcast files to iTunes and other podcast directories. You just upload your **FEED**, which is basically a list of links to your podcasts.

Since these directories are like search engines, you do need to make sure you add meta information to your podcasts to make it easy for people to find it. You can do this in iTunes, ID3 Editor, or many other software packages.

When you upload your podcast, you will need to add your title, keywords, your name (or pen name), your subtitle, a summary or description, and artwork that is between 1400x1400 and 3000x3000 pixels. You will also need one at 300x300.

Think of this image as your album cover. You want it to be eye-catching, visually appealing, and interesting to your target audience. Ideally, it will either have your face on it, or images that pertain to the subject material you discuss.

Once you upload your files and have a link to your feed, it's time to submit it to the various directories.

Here are some places you will want to submit your feed:

iTunes - Just launch iTunes on your Mac or PC, choose Podcasts from the menu at the top, click "Submit a Podcast" in the menu on the right, paste in your feed URL, and click "Continue".

Stitcher - Go to http://www.stitcher.com/content-providers and fill out the form. Click to agree to the Stitcher terms, and click "Continue".

Google Play - Go to
http://g.co/podcastportal and click "Get Started". use your Google account to log in and click "Add a Podcast". Accept their terms. Enter your feed. Check your email to verify ownership of the feed. Then click "Publish Podcast".

Other Services - There are other smaller services you might want to submit to later. I wouldn't worry too much about them in the beginning, but they can increase exposure, and every little bit helps.

Podcasting Success Strategies

You're almost there! You know pretty much everything you need to know to get started with podcasting. But now we're going to look at a few things you can do to take your podcasting to the next level.

Should You Use A Script?

Whether or not to use a script is a personal choice. I recommending trying to record one or two of each type without submitting them to directories, just to see which one works best for you.

Some people work better **with** a script, because they tend to stammer and stutter and have long periods of silence that must be edited out because they need time to think of what else they want to say.

Others work better **without** a script, because they find their speech sounds monotone or robotic as if they are reading something, because they are. Not everyone has the ability to read aloud naturally.

If you're doing an interview or group podcast, you might want to use a script just to make sure you both know what the material will be about before you start, and so there are no awkward periods while one of you, or both of you, need to think about what to say.

How Can You Find Listeners?

You will probably find a good number of listeners just through iTunes and other directories. As long as you're using proper keywords in your title and description, and you have an interesting concept and cover image, you will probably find listeners this way.

Another great way to find listeners is to conduct interviews with industry leaders or personalities. This will boost your views in directories by using their name, and it will also potentially get you some of their fans or followers because they will probably share a link to your podcast on their website or social media. It also helps you build your own credibility in the field.

Social media is also fantastic for gathering listeners. You can join and participate in groups and follow key players in your industry and link to your podcast.

A YouTube channel can also significantly boost your podcast listener base, and your podcast can significantly boost your YouTube viewership. It's a truly symbiotic relationship.

What Should You Talk About?

If you have trouble thinking of things to talk about for each episode, take a look at current podcasts in your niche, or check out YouTube videos or popular blogs to see what they are talking about and what people are interested in.

This is an easy way to see what is currently trending in the field, as well as giving you tons of ideas for topics!

Final Words

Podcasting is a great way to maximize your exposure, network with the leaders in your niche, and give your customers something extra in order to further brand awareness and connect with your target audience.

There's a lot less competition in podcasting than there is in blogging or creating videos as well, yet it's an incredible source of quality, free traffic that you should take advantage of.

Podcasting can bring in traffic to:

- Blogs

- Websites
- Ecommerce stores
- YouTube channels
- Social media profiles
- And lots more!

You don't need a lot of time or money to get started. You can often create a podcast and submit it in a couple of hours or less once you learn the process, and you probably already have a lot of what you need to begin.

There aren't many ways that are better at bringing in traffic with very little money or effort involved, so give it a try!

I wish you the best of luck!

Resources

Here are links to the resources found in this guide.

Audio Recording and Editing Tools:

TwistedWave

\>> https://twistedwave.com

Audacity

\>> http://audacity.sourceforge.net/

Podcast Hosting:

Libsyn

>> http://libsyn.com

Buzzsprout

>> http://buzzsprout.com

Podcast Directories:

Stitcher

>> http://www.stitcher.com/content-providers

Google Play

>> http://g.co/podcastportal

www.ingramcontent.com/pod-product-compliance
Lightning Source LLC
Chambersburg PA
CBHW070903070326
40690CB00009B/1972